EQUIPPING SAINTS FOR SERVICE

HOW

MISSION READY
IS REDEFINING REMOTE
VILLAGE
EVANGELISM

Robert JC Morgan

**EQUIPPING SAINTS FOR SERVICE: HOW MISSION READY IS
REDEFINING REMOTE VILLAGE EVANGELISM**
By Robert JC Morgan

Photography: Corinne Morgan & Nicholas Morgan
Cover Design: Cari Campbell, Cari Campbell Design
Interior Design: Shiloh Schroeder, Fusion Creative Works
Primary Editor: Kim Foster
Project Managers: Kelly Cope, Jacob Barrett, Maryanna Young, and Hannah Cross

ISBN: 978-1-61206-073-6

First Printing
Published in the United States of America
Printed in Canada
Published by:

Boise, Idaho

www.AlohaPublishing.com
ALL PROCEEDS FROM BOOK SALES GO TO MISSION READY, INC., TO SUPPORT REMOTE VILLAGE EVANGELISM ACTIVITIES.
www.MissionReady.org

GREETINGS, AND THANK YOU FOR SUPPORTING MISSION READY
THROUGH YOUR PURCHASE OF THIS PHOTO BOOK.

My name is Robert Morgan, and I would like to personally invite you to join me in the great adventure of serving the Lord in beautiful and remote regions of the developing world.

In 2005, I felt the Lord encouraging me to start an organization whose focus would be to support and equip men and women seeking to answer God's call to Christian missionary service in the most remote places on the planet.

Mission Ready's focus is an area known as the "10–40 Window," a band of countries between 10 and 40 degrees north latitude, from western Africa through Asia. This area includes 35 percent of the world's land mass, 90 percent of the world's poorest peoples, and 95 percent of those who have yet to hear the great truth of salvation through Jesus Christ's sacrifice in atonement for our sin.

I never imagined the Lord would lead me to personally come alongside of these brave missionaries as they endure the hardships of trekking up mountains and through jungles to bring the good news of the gospel to remote peoples . . . yet this has become a treasured part of my life.

By sharing these pictures and stories from my travels, I hope to inspire you to fall in love with our brothers and sisters living in these remote places, just as I have. Furthermore, I trust that the Lord will turn your love into action and lead you to join this great campaign by supporting Remote Village Evangelism through both your prayers and financial support.

All donations to Mission Ready, Inc. are tax deductible under current IRS guidelines.

For more information, or to support Mission Ready please visit our website at www.MissionReady.org.

AND [JESUS] SAID TO THEM,

"Whoever receives this little child in My name
receives Me; and whoever receives Me
receives Him who sent me."

– Luke 9:48a

The landscape is harsh and life is difficult for most Ethiopians.
It is common for people to walk up to eight hours each day in their search to provide for their families.

Yea, though I walk through the valley of the shadow of death,
I will fear no evil; for You are with me; Your rod and Your staff, they comfort me. – Psalm 23:4

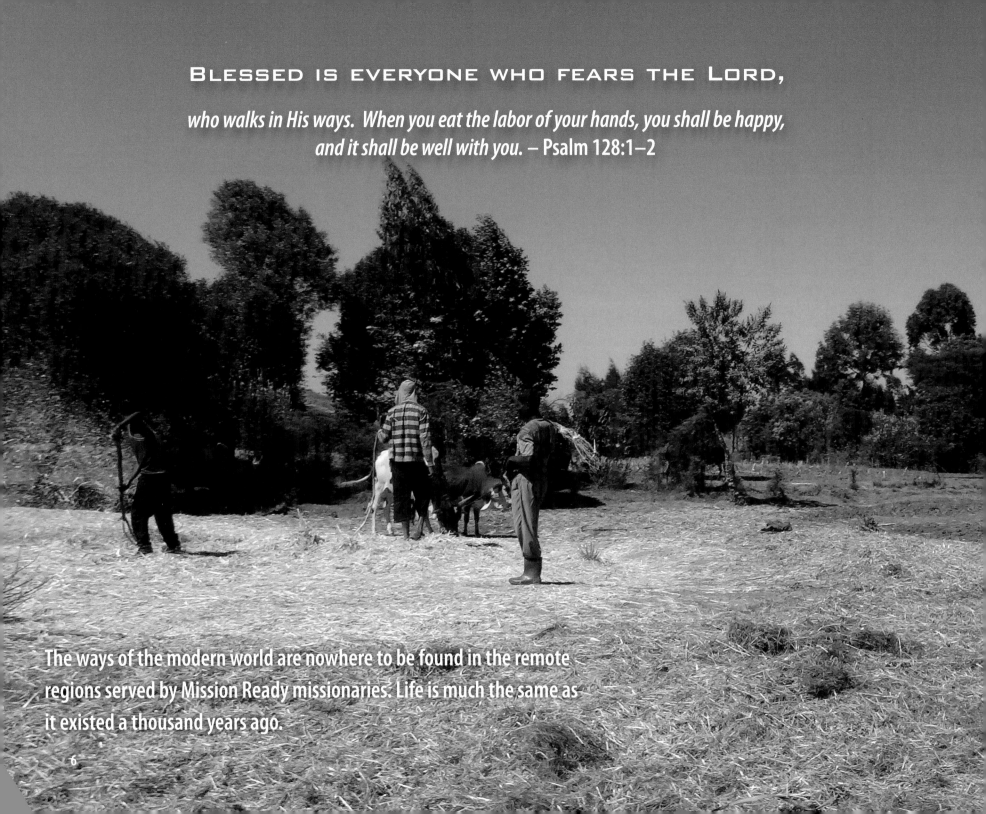

BLESSED IS EVERYONE WHO FEARS THE LORD,

who walks in His ways. When you eat the labor of your hands, you shall be happy, and it shall be well with you. – Psalm 128:1–2

The ways of the modern world are nowhere to be found in the remote regions served by Mission Ready missionaries. Life is much the same as it existed a thousand years ago.

While the earth remains, seedtime and harvest, cold and heat, winter and summer, and day and night shall not cease.
– Genesis 8:22

Our missionaries engage people wherever they find them . . . in their villages, homes, and places of work.

THEN HE SAID TO HIS DISCIPLES,

"The harvest truly is plentiful, but the laborers are few.
Therefore pray the Lord of the harvest to send
out laborers into His harvest."
– Matthew 9:37–38

As we move further away from the cities and into the countryside, shops are replaced by street-side barter.

AND BEHOLD,
THE LORD STOOD ABOVE IT AND SAID:

"I am the LORD God of Abraham your father and the God of Isaac; the land on which you lie I will give to you and your descendants. Also your descendants shall be as the dust of the earth; you shall spread abroad to the west and the east, to the north and the south; and in you and in your seed all the families of the earth shall be blessed."

– Genesis 28:13–14

AND JESUS CAME AND SPOKE TO THEM, SAYING,

"All authority has been given to Me in heaven and on earth. Go therefore and make disciples of all the nations, baptizing them in the name of the Father and of the Son and of the Holy Spirit, teaching them to observe all things that I have commanded you; and lo, I am with you always, even to the end of the age." Amen.

– Matthew 28:18–20

This young girl will hear the good news of the Christian gospels because God has blessed the sacrificial efforts of Christian missionaries and provided them with support through the generosity of people just like you.

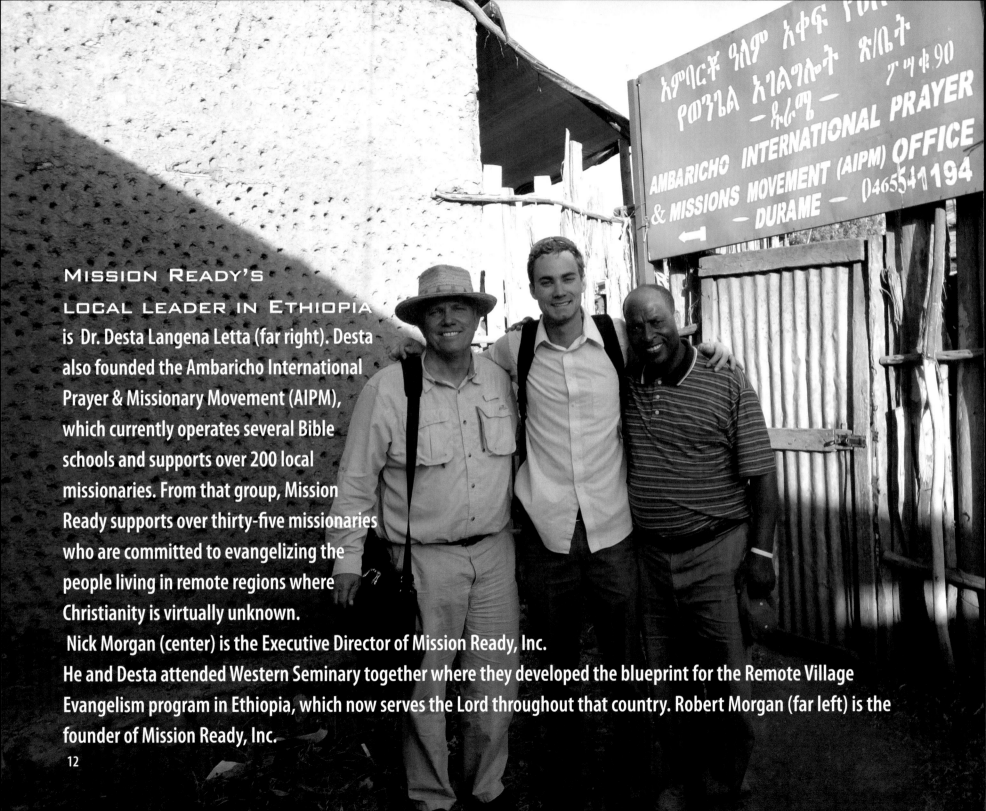

MISSION READY'S LOCAL LEADER IN ETHIOPIA is Dr. Desta Langena Letta (far right). Desta also founded the Ambaricho International Prayer & Missionary Movement (AIPM), which currently operates several Bible schools and supports over 200 local missionaries. From that group, Mission Ready supports over thirty-five missionaries who are committed to evangelizing the people living in remote regions where Christianity is virtually unknown.

Nick Morgan (center) is the Executive Director of Mission Ready, Inc. He and Desta attended Western Seminary together where they developed the blueprint for the Remote Village Evangelism program in Ethiopia, which now serves the Lord throughout that country. Robert Morgan (far left) is the founder of Mission Ready, Inc.

MY WORDS COME FROM MY UPRIGHT HEART;

my lips utter pure knowledge.
The Spirit of God has made me,
and the breath of the Almighty gives me life.
– Job 33:3–4

Mission Ready's purpose is "Equipping saints for service." We support local, indigenous pastors and missionaries who are familiar with the cultures, languages, and hardships of the remote regions in which they serve. Here, missionaries attend rigorous Bible training to ensure they are equipped with sound theological knowledge before being accepted into the Remote Village Evangelism program.

One unique aspect of our missionary support program is its ability to prepare

and equip local pastors and missionaries at a relatively low cost through the use of local indigenous resources.

For example, this Bible school serves an entire geographic region.

Mission Ready recognizes and respects the value and contribution of all Christian missionaries. One of our early epiphanies, however, was to recognize that God is also lifting up many local people in these remote regions and giving them the desire to participate in Christian evangelism.

Our research indicates that to support and equip one missionary from the United States for remote village evangelism can cost as much as $75,000 per year.

Once these missionaries arrive "in country," they often struggle to overcome the hardships of culture, language, disease, and harsh living conditions.

In stark contrast, we are able to prepare and support local, indigenous missionaries for less than $2,000 per year.

This allows Mission Ready to place thirty-seven missionaries in the field with the same resource commitment required to support a single US missionary.

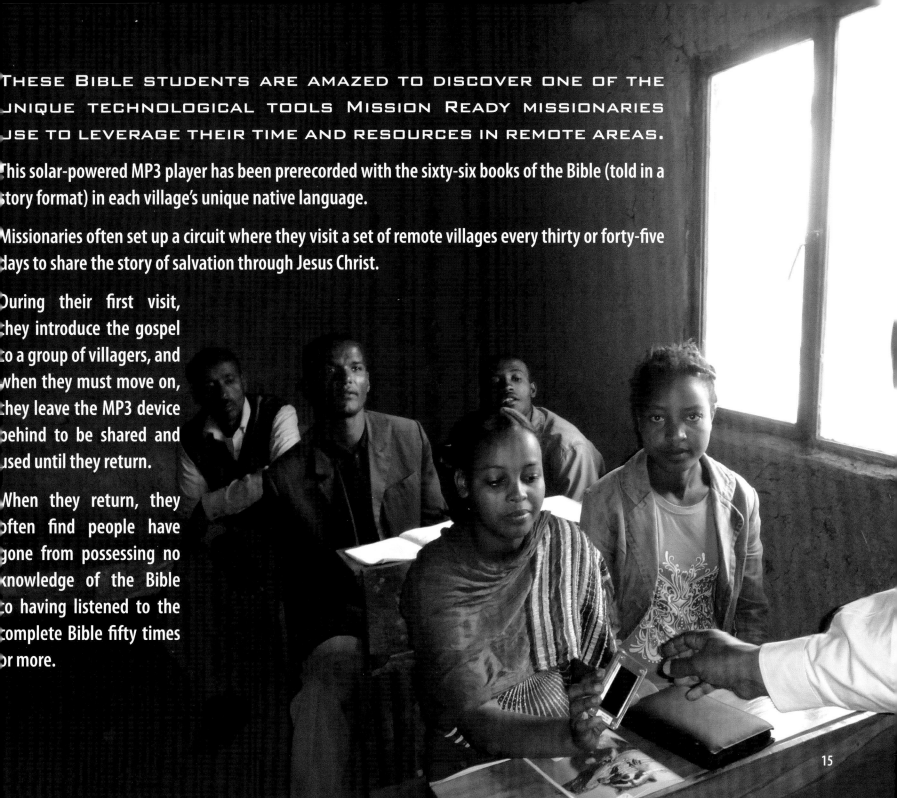

THESE BIBLE STUDENTS ARE AMAZED TO DISCOVER ONE OF THE UNIQUE TECHNOLOGICAL TOOLS MISSION READY MISSIONARIES USE TO LEVERAGE THEIR TIME AND RESOURCES IN REMOTE AREAS.

This solar-powered MP3 player has been prerecorded with the sixty-six books of the Bible (told in a story format) in each village's unique native language.

Missionaries often set up a circuit where they visit a set of remote villages every thirty or forty-five days to share the story of salvation through Jesus Christ.

During their first visit, they introduce the gospel to a group of villagers, and when they must move on, they leave the MP3 device behind to be shared and used until they return.

When they return, they often find people have gone from possessing no knowledge of the Bible to having listened to the complete Bible fifty times or more.

15

BUT YOU BE WATCHFUL IN ALL THINGS,

endure afflictions,
do the work of an evangelist,
fulfill your ministry.
– 2 Timothy 4:5

Nick Morgan encourages a group of missionaries who endure great hardship daily to share their faith.

THE LORD IS YOUR KEEPER; *the LORD is your shade at your right hand. The sun shall not strike you by day, nor the moon by night. – Psalm 121:5–6*

In this remote village, missionaries gather to share the good news of the gospel under the shade of the "Story Tree."

18

UNDER THE SHADE OF THE STORY TREE, this man told an inspirational story of how he had spent over fifty years in isolation as the only Christian believer in this remote region.

During much of that time, he was persecuted, beaten, and ostracized from the community for his belief.

He shared that even in his darkest hour, the Lord gave him strength, hope, and a belief that one day others would come to know the Lord, and he would spend his final days in the Christian community he so longed for all his life.

A few years ago, God answered his prayers and now their small enclave of a dozen huts has become the community of believers he had prayed for over all those years.

I WAITED PATIENTLY FOR THE LORD;

And He inclined to me,
And heard my cry.
– Psalm 40:1

WHEN THE MESSENGERS OF JOHN HAD DEPARTED,

He [Jesus] began to speak to the multitudes concerning John: "What did you go out into the wilderness to see? A reed shaken by the wind?"
– Luke 7:24

This photo is representative of the dwellings and living conditions found in remote Ethiopia. These are the people Mission Ready missionaries seek to reach with the message of God's great love and salvation through Jesus Christ's atonement for the sins of the world.

WHOSE HOME I HAVE MADE THE WILDERNESS,
AND THE BARREN LAND HIS DWELLING?
– JOB 39:6

THE CHILDREN OF ETHIOPIA, like children everywhere, enjoy playing with friends in the sunshine and dreaming of a future where they can go to school and learn the skills necessary to live a better life.

AND NOW, LITTLE CHILDREN, ABIDE IN HIM,

that when He appears, we may have confidence and not be ashamed before Him at His coming.
– 1 John 2:28

THE LORD CONFUSED THE LANGUAGE OF ALL THE EARTH;

and from there (Babel) the Lord scattered them abroad over the face of all the earth.
– Genesis 11:9

A missionary shares audio stories from the Bible with a village family. They are all curious to know how this machine can speak to them in their own language.

Missionaries gather outside the original church built by AIPM in the southern region. They have worked for several years to establish a Christian community in this non-Christian region and must remain vigilant, as their presence has not yet been accepted and they frequently experience persecution. Their crops have been burned four years in a row, they have endured beatings, and their compound has been attacked with gunfire and fire bombs. Still, they remain joyful in their work and praise God continuously for protecting and sustaining them in this hostile land.

FOR IF WE LIVE, WE LIVE TO THE LORD;

and if we die, we die to the Lord. Therefore, whether we live or die, we are the Lord's.
– Romans 14:8

NOW IT HAPPENED AS THEY JOURNEYED ON THE ROAD, THAT SOMEONE SAID TO HIM,

"Lord, I will follow You wherever You go." And Jesus said to him, "Foxes have holes and birds of the air have nests, but the Son of Man has nowhere to lay His head." – Luke 9:57–58

Sometimes the only way we could tell the road from the wilderness was by the cactus lining its path.

In this remote southeast region of Ethiopia,

the Mission Ready Remote Evangelism Team was blessed to play a role in building a new Christian church in an area with no prior Christian presence.

Some of the members of this new congregation walked for days to be a part of this church raising.

To see the pure joy on their faces was to catch a small glimpse of heaven.

Even in the most remote places, Ethiopians make time to enjoy coffee. It is a rich part of their culture and heritage and one of the ways they make their guests feel welcome. Here, I enjoy a cup in the traditional way, with salt and butter.

DO NOT FORGET TO ENTERTAIN STRANGERS, *for by so doing some have unwittingly entertained angels.*
– Hebrews 13:2

27

BUT JESUS CALLED TO HIM AND SAID,

"Let the little children come to Me, and do not forbid them; for of such is the kingdom of God. Assuredly, I say to you, whoever does not receive the kingdom of God as a little child will by no means enter it." – Luke 18:16–17

Occasionally Ethiopia's harsh landscape is blessed by a lake or river.
It is a beautiful sight for weary travelers at the end of a long day walking hot dusty roads.

THE LORD IS MY SHEPHERD;
I SHALL NOT WANT.

He makes me to lie down in green pastures;
He leads me beside the still waters.
He restores my soul.
– Psalm 23:1–3a

HE WHO BELIEVES IN ME,

as the Scripture has said, out of his heart will flow rivers of living water.

– John 7:38

Water equates to life in Ethiopia. It is such a scarce commodity that people make the most of it wherever it is found.

IT IS EASIER FOR A CAMEL TO GO
THROUGH THE EYE OF A NEEDLE

than for a rich man to enter the kingdom of God.
– Mark 10:25

Seeing camels running wild reminded me that I was very, very far from home . . . a guest in a foreign land.

GOD'S AMAZING GRACE IS EVIDENT in the story of this village church. The man standing was a successful farmer and community leader. Years ago he donated land for a mosque and was made a powerful sheik. A traveling missionary shared the Christian gospel with this sheik's son, who then defied his family and accepted Christ. The sheik initially banished the son and refused to hear the gospel message.

32

OVER TIME, THE SON SECRETLY SHARED the gospel with his brothers and sisters who also came to know the Lord. The sheik, fearing that his family was in crisis, finally agreed to listen to the message brought by the Christian missionaries. Upon hearing the Word, the sheik's cold heart melted and he too accepted the Lord. He tore down the mosque and replaced it with this Christian church on the same site. Now, he and his entire family are the "end of the spear," bringing this new message of salvation through Jesus Christ to this entire region.

And I also say to you that you are Peter, and on this rock I will build My church, and the gates of Hades shall not prevail against it. – Matthew 16:18

THE COURAGEOUS MEMBERS OF THIS CONGREGATION COME TOGETHER IN A SHOW OF UNITY.

Desta introduces another group of missionaries to Mission Ready's solar-powered MP3 player. They are anxious to begin using it to supplement their evangelism efforts in the surrounding villages.

The LORD will cause His glorious voice to be heard.
— Isaiah 30:30a

35

THE PEOPLE
WHO **WALKED** IN
DARKNESS HAVE
SEEN A GREAT **LIGHT**;
THOSE WHO **DWELT** IN
THE LAND OF THE
SHADOW OF **DEATH**,
UPON THEM A **LIGHT**
HAS **SHINED**.
– ISAIAH 9:2

As our journey continues, we must leave this young Christian outpost in God's loving care.

We are moved by the faith of these courageous people and the knowledge that God's amazing grace knows no geographical boundary.

We feel blessed to have played even a small part in God's plan for these wonderful brothers and sisters in the Spirit.

We are humbled that the Lord is using Mission Ready in a powerful way to encourage and support these brave new Christian communities.

Then He will give the rain for your seed with which you sow the ground, and bread of the increase of the earth; it will be fat and plentiful. In that day your cattle will feed in large pastures.
— Isaiah 30:23

In the heat of the Ethiopian summer, pasture is scarce and cattle are lean.

Here is what I have seen:

It is good and fitting for one to eat and drink, and to enjoy the good of all his labor in which he toils under the sun all the days of his life which God gives him; for it is his heritage.

– Ecclesiastes 5:18

Occasionally our travels take us through small towns where the hustle and bustle
are a welcome change from the isolation and loneliness of the remote regions.

Sing, O heavens! Be joyful, O earth! And break out in singing, O mountains! For the LORD has comforted His people, and will have mercy on His afflicted.
– Isaiah 49:13

One of the most amazing and inspirational experiences of my life was participating in a Christian pilgrimage to the top of Ambaricho, mountain. This mountain rises almost 11,000 feet above the southern Ethiopia landscape and was a center of pagan satanic worship for generations. In the 1930s, missionaries brought the Christian gospel to the animistic Kambatta people living there, but war soon forced these missionaries to leave, and persecution of new believers was severe. Still the gospel spread and the church grew through the bold witness of committed Ethiopian Christians. Under Communist rule from 1974–1990, the gospel was outlawed and many evangelists (including Desta) were imprisoned and tortured. In prison, some found comfort in the power of prayer, and when freedom came, these prayer warriors began claiming mountains like Ambaricho for the Lord. In this current generation, the former "witch doctors" have accepted Christ as their Lord and Savior, and this mountain has been transformed into a prayer mountain where over 100,000 Christians come together each January to participate in a day of prayer and worship.

This quaint mountain church, which is perched 8,000 feet above sea level, serves as base camp for our Ambaricho mountain ascent.

Sing to the LORD with thanksgiving;
sing praises on the harp to our God, Who covers the heavens with clouds,
Who prepares rain for the earth, Who makes grass to grow on the mountains.
– Psalm 147:7–8

For we, though many,
are one bread and one body;
for we all partake of that one bread.
— 1 Corinthians 10:17

Upon our arrival, we are treated to a traditional breakfast of injera and goat stew, which local pastors have prepared for us.

41

THEREFORE, WHETHER YOU EAT OR DRINK, or whatever you do, do all to the glory of God.
– 1 Corinthians 10:31

We are also treated to Ethiopian coffee . . . with butter and salt of course.

42

THEN YOU SHALL RETURN TO THE LAND OF YOUR POSSESSION and enjoy it, which Moses the LORD's servant gave you on this side of the Jordan toward the sunrise.
– Joshua 1:15b

Our ascent begins at sunrise as a beautiful clear day dawns on the mountain.

LIKE ARROWS IN THE HAND OF A
WARRIOR, SO ARE THE CHILDREN
OF ONE'S YOUTH. – PSALM 127:4

Local mountain children run from
their houses to greet us along the way.

44

These women rush to show us their treasured Bible and encourage us on our climb.

BUT THE ANGEL ANSWERED
AND SAID TO THE WOMEN,
"Do not be afraid, for I know that you seek Jesus
who was crucified." – Matthew 28:5

I am determined to complete this pilgrimage, even though the trail up the mountain was much more difficult than I expected. At this altitude, the air is so thin I struggle to breathe with every step I take.

NOT THAT I HAVE ALREADY ATTAINED,

or am already perfected; but I press on, that I may lay hold of that for which Christ Jesus has also laid hold of me.
– Philippians 3:12

ALONG THE TRAIL, WE COME UPON AN ANCIENT CEMETERY. A local pastor, with whom I am climbing, provides some humorous motivation by telling me that this is where the people who do not complete the climb are laid to rest.

DO NOT MARVEL AT THIS; for the hour is coming in which all who are in the graves will hear His voice and come forth—those who have done good, to the resurrection of life, and those who have done evil, to the resurrection of condemnation.
– John 5:28–29

47

NOW IT SHALL COME TO PASS IN THE LATTER DAYS

that the mountain of the LORD's house shall be established on the top of the mountains, and shall be exalted above the hills; and all nations shall flow to it. — Isaiah 2:2

TRIUMPHANTLY I REACH THE SUMMIT OF THE MOUNTAIN
(about an hour after the others in my party), and my eyes behold a truly amazing sight!

Now great multitudes went with Him. And He turned and said to them,

"If anyone comes to Me and does not hate his father and mother, wife and children, brothers and sisters, yes, and his own life also, he cannot be My disciple."
– Luke 14:25–26

A great multitude of modern-day Christians has gathered to worship the King of Kings and Lord of Lords.

THE NOISE OF A MULTITUDE IN THE MOUNTAINS, *like that of many people! A tumultuous noise of the kingdoms of nations gathered together! The LORD of hosts musters the army for battle. — Isaiah 13:4*

On this makeshift stage of dirt and branches, we bow to praise the Lord and dedicate this event to His honor and glory.

THE SPEAKERS, RISING ABOVE THIS GATHERING ON BAMBOO POLES,

... Multiple Ready "equipping saints for service" by providing AIPM with this sound system. This ... first time, to communicate effectively with the multitude of believers ... Ambaricho Mountain for this holy day of prayer.

51

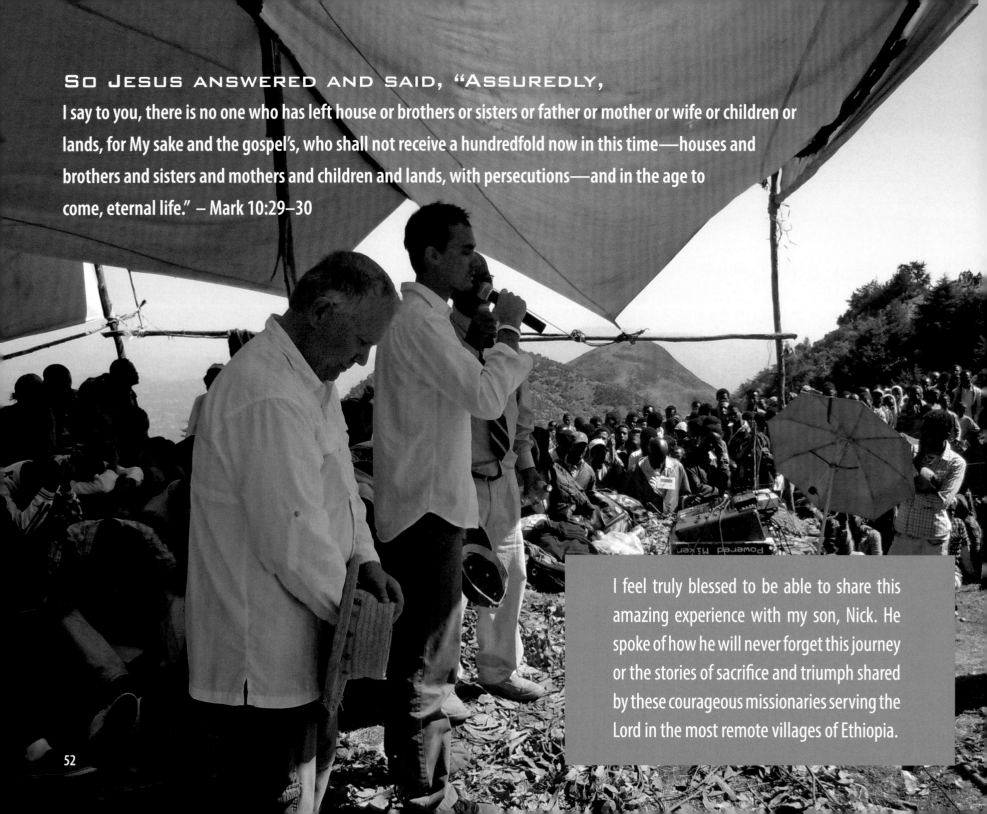

So Jesus answered and said, "Assuredly,
I say to you, there is no one who has left house or brothers or sisters or father or mother or wife or children or lands, for My sake and the gospel's, who shall not receive a hundredfold now in this time—houses and brothers and sisters and mothers and children and lands, with persecutions—and in the age to come, eternal life." – Mark 10:29–30

I feel truly blessed to be able to share this amazing experience with my son, Nick. He spoke of how he will never forget this journey or the stories of sacrifice and triumph shared by these courageous missionaries serving the Lord in the most remote villages of Ethiopia.

ALL THE EARTH SHALL WORSHIP YOU AND SING PRAISES TO YOU;
they shall sing praises to Your name. Selah. – Psalm 66:4

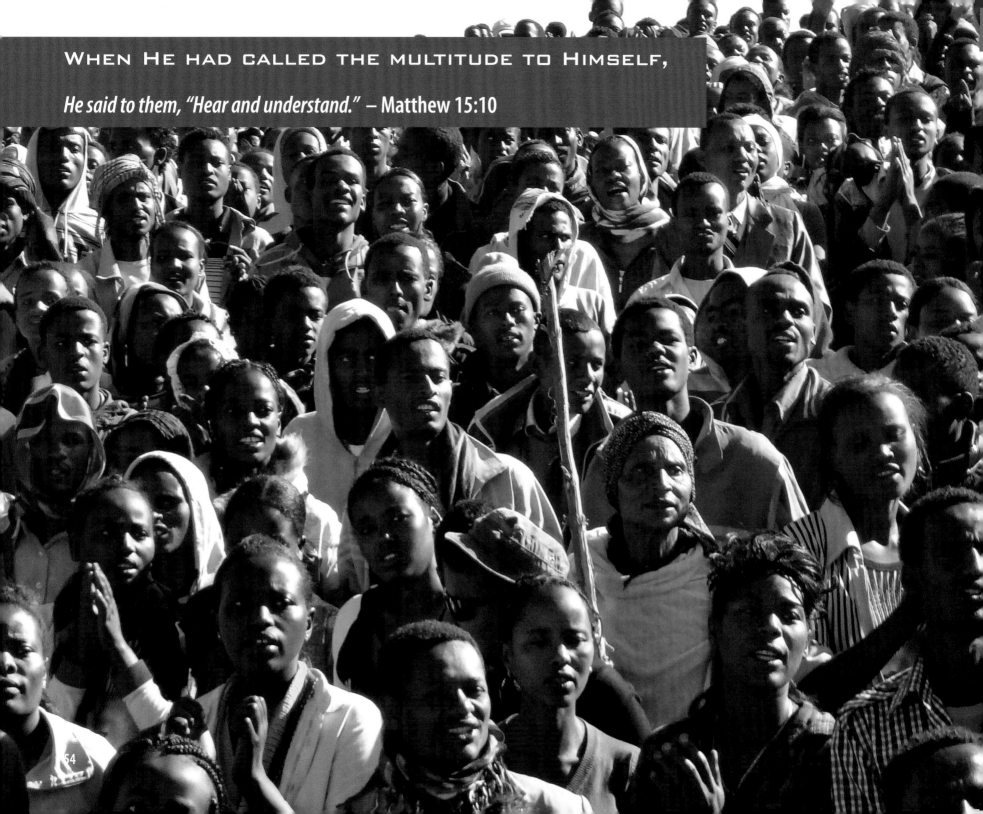

WHEN HE HAD CALLED THE MULTITUDE TO HIMSELF,

He said to them, "Hear and understand." – Matthew 15:10

54

ENVOYS WILL COME OUT OF EGYPT;
Ethiopia will quickly stretch out her hands to God.
– Psalm 68:31

NOW AN ANGEL OF THE LORD SPOKE TO PHILIP, SAYING, "Arise and go toward the south along the road which goes down from Jerusalem to Gaza." This is desert. So he arose and went. And behold, a man of Ethiopia, a eunuch of great authority under Candace the queen of the Ethiopians, who had charge of all her treasury, and had come to Jerusalem to worship, was returning. And sitting in his chariot, he was reading Isaiah the prophet.

— Acts 8:26–28

THE GENEROUS SOUL WILL BE MADE RICH, and he who waters will also be watered himself.

– Proverbs 11:25

While descending the mountain after the day of prayer and worship came to an end, we are invited into the home of a kind and generous family.

We are inspired by this couple's hospitality and generosity of spirit, as they joyfully welcome us and share with us what little provisions they have.

So the churches were strengthened in the faith, *and increased in number daily.* – Acts 16:5

As our journey is coming to a close, we cannot leave Ethiopia without visiting one last church congregation. We travel for hours on roads that could scarcely be called trails. As the sun sets, we finally arrive at our final Christian outpost—the very first church started by Mission Ready missionaries in Ethiopia.

THEREFORE TAKE HEED TO YOURSELVES AND TO ALL THE FLOCK, among which the Holy Spirit has made you overseers, to shepherd the church of God which He purchased with His own blood. – Acts 20:28

MISSION READY WORKS WITH LOCAL PASTORS AND MISSIONARIES IN GHANA, Africa, who are called to conduct Remote Village Evangelism.

This area is more tropical than Ethiopia and presents its own unique challenges.

These are some of the men and women who work tirelessly to share the gospel message throughout Ghana.

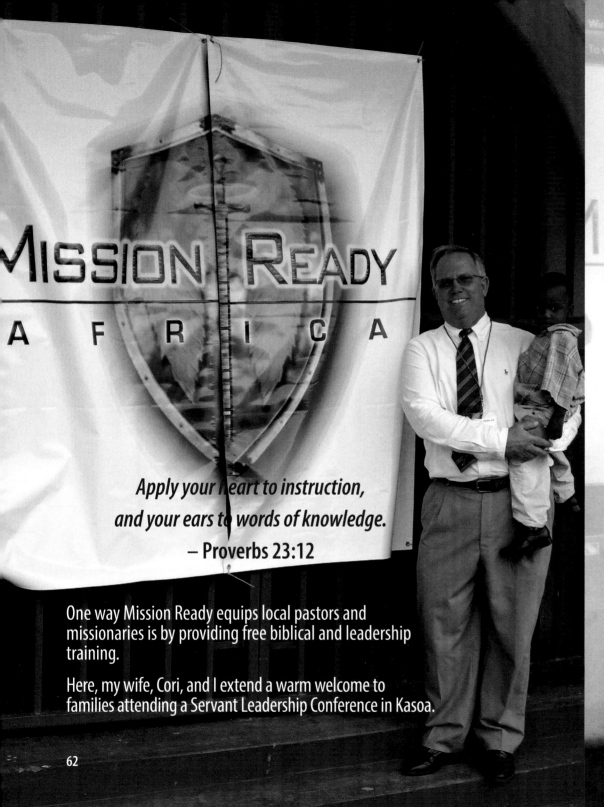

*Apply your heart to instruction,
and your ears to words of knowledge.*
– Proverbs 23:12

One way Mission Ready equips local pastors and missionaries is by providing free biblical and leadership training.

Here, my wife, Cori, and I extend a warm welcome to families attending a Servant Leadership Conference in Kasoa.

There is a great hunger among missionaries, pastors, and church leaders to receive leadership training. We expect two dozen participants and more than 300 arrive, many traveling great distances to be a part of this three-day training experience.

For I know the thoughts that I think toward you, says the LORD, thoughts of peace and not of evil, to give you a future and a hope.
– Jeremiah 29:11

The heart of the prudent acquires knowledge, and the ear of the wise seeks knowledge.
– Proverbs 18:15

WE MAKE OUR CONFERENCES "FAMILY FRIENDLY" in the hope that God may be planting the seeds of inspiration in the hearts of these youngsters. Perhaps they will become this nation's future missionaries.

64

LITTLE CHILDREN, LET NO ONE DECEIVE YOU.

He who practices righteousness is righteous,
just as He is righteous.
– 1 John 3:7

We also enjoy visiting local schools and encouraging the children to view their education as a wonderful gift of God. The headmaster of this school in Kasoa is a Mission Ready missionary.

SOON IT IS TIME TO LEAVE THE CITY and pursue the work for which we are called, visiting the most remote villages where few have gone before us.

66

But as for you, brethren, do not grow weary in doing good.
— 2 Thessalonians 3:13

We travel by vehicle
for as long as
possible . . .
although at times even finding fuel
can prove to be an adventure.

For I was hungry
and you gave Me food;
I was thirsty and you gave Me drink;
I was a stranger and you took Me in.
– Matthew 25:35

When hungry, we are blessed
by the hospitality of strangers
who share the little food they have.

When the roads end or the fuel runs out,

we complete the journey on foot.

Here, Pastor Judah and Pastor Eric walk the dusty road to deliver the good news of Jesus.

Go therefore and make disciples of all the nations,

baptizing them in the name of the Father and of the Son and of the Holy Spirit.
— Matthew 28:19

This is the much revered King and Chief of Gomoa, Ohua. He is the first tribal leader to allow Mission Ready missionaries to hold evangelism crusades in his village.

NO KING IS SAVED BY THE MULTITUDE OF AN ARMY;
a mighty man is not delivered by great strength.
– Psalm 33:16

IT WAS AT THE FIRST NIGHT CRUSADE I EVER ATTENDED THAT I WAS BLESSED TO WATCH THIS NOBLE KING GIVE HIS LIFE TO JESUS.

He then spent the rest of his days leading his people out of idol worship and into a relationship with the Lord.

MISSION READY'S PURPOSE IS
SOMEWHAT UNIQUE IN THAT
WE NEVER SEEK TO REPLACE
THE LOCAL CHRISTIAN
CHURCH.

Rather, we seek to train and equip local pastors to better share the message of salvation with their own people.

Here a local pastor shares the Word with a crowd in a night crusade.

Night programs are popular because many more people can attend, and it avoids the oppressive heat of the day.

IF WE SAY THAT WE HAVE FELLOWSHIP WITH HIM, *and walk in darkness, we lie and do not practice the truth. But if we walk in the light as He is in the light, we have fellowship with one another, and the blood of Jesus Christ His Son cleanses us from all sin.*

– 1 John 1:6 –7

MISSION READY ENJOYS MAKING CREATIVE USE OF TECHNOLOGY IN THE REMOTE VILLAGE EVANGELISM PROGRAMS.

Here, a group gathers for "Movie Night" in a remote village.

Missionaries pack in a small generator, a projector, and an old bed sheet on which to show Christian music videos and Christian movies. At each intermission, they share messages from the Bible with the crowd.

UNTO THE UPRIGHT THERE ARISES LIGHT IN THE DARKNESS;

He is gracious, and full of compassion, and righteous.
– Psalm 112:4

BLESSED IS HE WHO CONSIDERS THE POOR;

the LORD will deliver him in time of trouble.
– Psalm 41:1

Over time, a special relationship has developed between Mission Ready and the people of the remote village of Gomoa, Ohua.
With their support, several "pilot programs" have been launched, which brings education, nutrition, and better living conditions to these people.

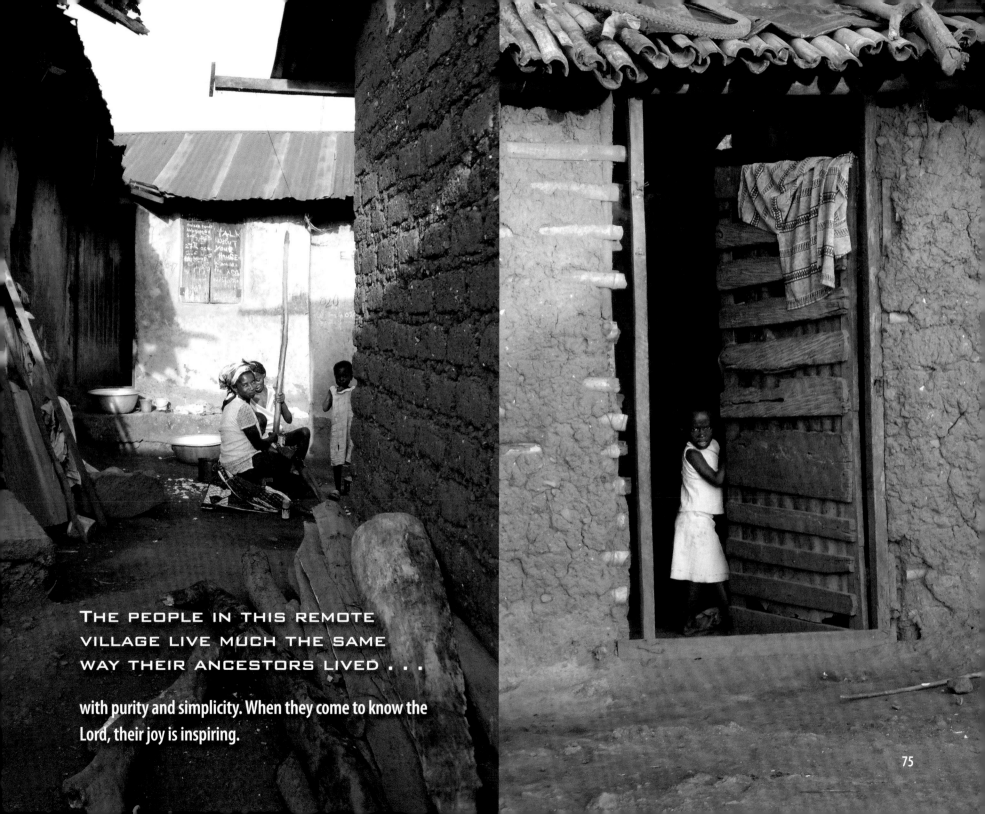

THE PEOPLE IN THIS REMOTE
VILLAGE LIVE MUCH THE SAME
WAY THEIR ANCESTORS LIVED . . .

with purity and simplicity. When they come to know the
Lord, their joy is inspiring.

WE BRING THE KNOWLEDGE OF
SALVATION THROUGH CHRIST

to these remote people, so they can make informed
decisions about their own futures.

THE LORD IS MY ROCK
AND MY FORTRESS
AND MY DELIVERER;

my God, my strength, in whom I will trust;
my shield and the horn of my salvation,
my stronghold.
– Psalm 18:2

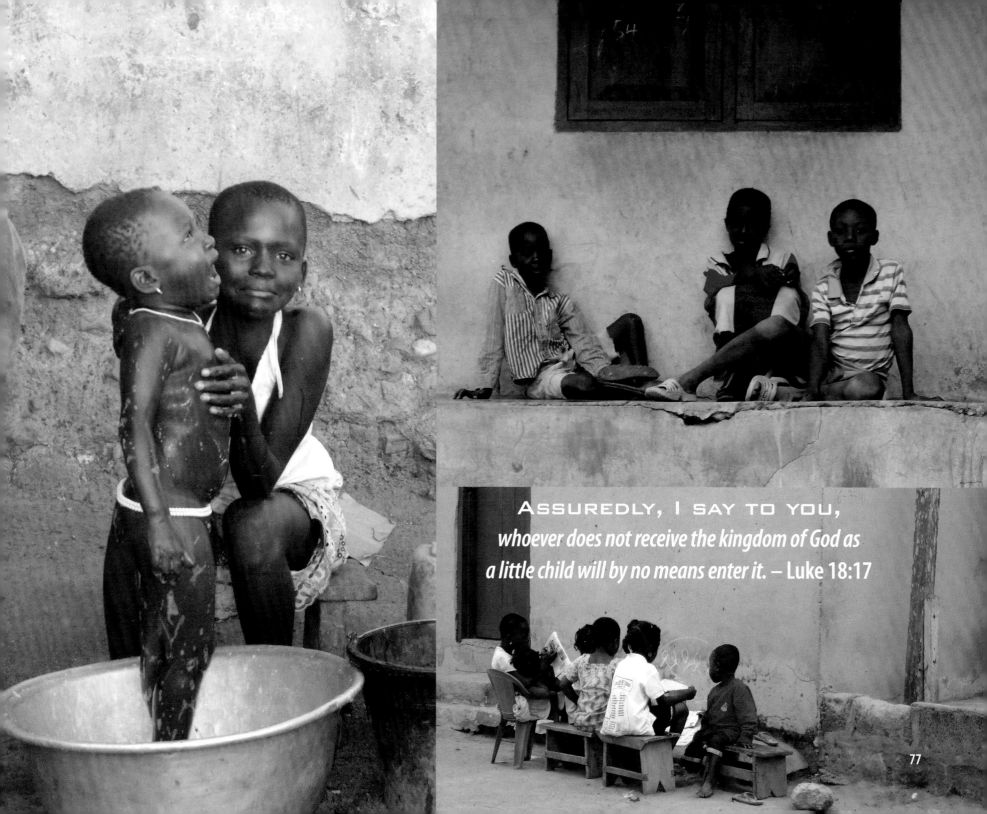

ASSUREDLY, I SAY TO YOU,
whoever does not receive the kingdom of God as
a little child will by no means enter it. – Luke 18:17

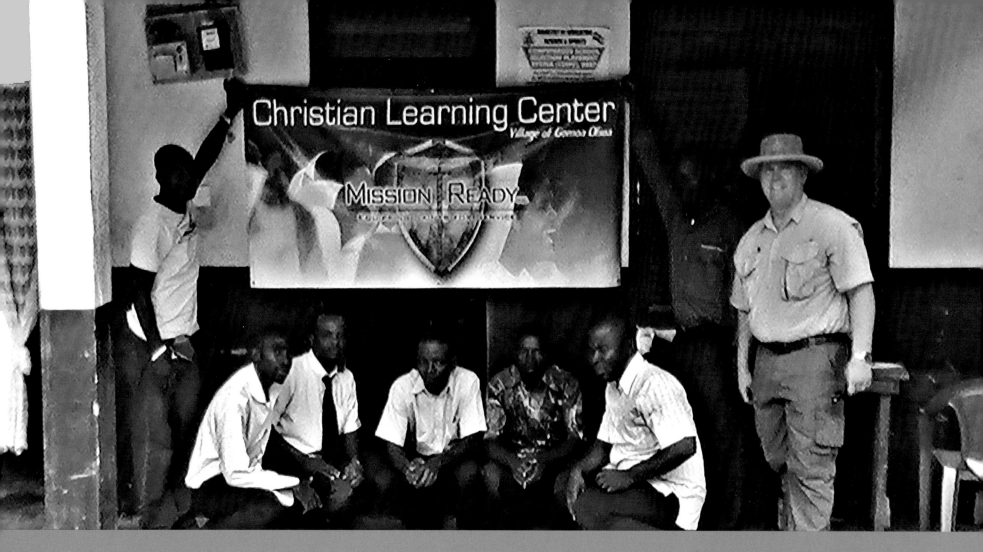

IN THIS OPEN-AIR "GOVERNMENT SCHOOL," HUNDREDS OF CHILDREN RECEIVE THEIR ONLY EDUCATION. MISSION READY ANSWERED A CALL TO HELP THIS NEXT GENERATION BETTER ACHIEVE THEIR POTENTIAL.

With the help of the community, Mission Ready established a Christian Learning Center equipped with ten computers and Christian educational software for grades K–12 to supplement the education provided by the government school in Gomoa, Ohua.

This was the first time most of the 600-plus village children had ever seen a computer, and these are the only computers to be found anywhere within a 50-mile radius of the village.

THUS SAYS THE LORD OF HOSTS:

"Old men and old women shall again sit in the streets of Jerusalem, each one with his staff in his hand because of great age"
– Zechariah 8:4

MISSION READY ALSO ESTABLISHED A GOAT RANCHING PROJECT IN THE VILLAGE THAT IS DESIGNED to teach Christian business concepts and generate much needed revenue to help pay for basic human services. Excess milk from the goat ranching operation is provided free to village children as an early nutrition program. The goat ranch is designed to bring immediate value to the people of the village and provides a natural opportunity for local pastors to work together and teach biblical concepts.

MISSION READY ALSO PROVIDES free advanced biblical training to local pastors and missionaries through a distance learning program developed in part by a professor at Western Seminary in Portland, Oregon.

Local open-air churches like this serve as the venue used by Mission Ready to provide sound Bible training to aspiring missionaries and pastors planning to serve in remote areas.

REMEMBER THE DAYS OF OLD,

Consider the years of many generations.
Ask your father, and he will show you;
Your elders, and they will tell you.
— Deuteronomy 32:7

The Queen Mother of Gomoa, Ohua (far right) became a strong supporter of Mission Ready.
She accepted Christ as her personal Savior before her unexpected death in 2012.

THEREFORE WITH JOY YOU *will draw water from the wells of salvation.*
– Isaiah 12:3

Each morning, the young girls of the village bring water for use in the school.

WE TRAVEL TO AS MANY VILLAGES THAT WILL ALLOW US IN TO TELL THE GOOD NEWS OF THE GOSPEL.

In each village, we must first receive the approval of the king before we are allowed to evangelize his people.

We must also tell him the story of the things we saw on our journey to his village.

In each place we visit, we ask to pray for the sick and elderly and those in need of God's provision.

AND THE PRAYER OF FAITH WILL SAVE THE SICK, and the Lord will raise him up. And if he has committed sins, he will be forgiven.

— James 5:15

THE MISSIONARIES SPEND AS MUCH TIME AS POSSIBLE
meeting people and praying with them wherever they are.

We use prayer as a means to explain to people that we are all children of a loving God, and He desires to have a personal relationship with each of us through Christ Jesus.

THEREFORE I EXHORT FIRST OF ALL THAT SUPPLICATIONS, *prayers, intercessions, and giving of thanks be made for all men. — 1 Timothy 2:1*

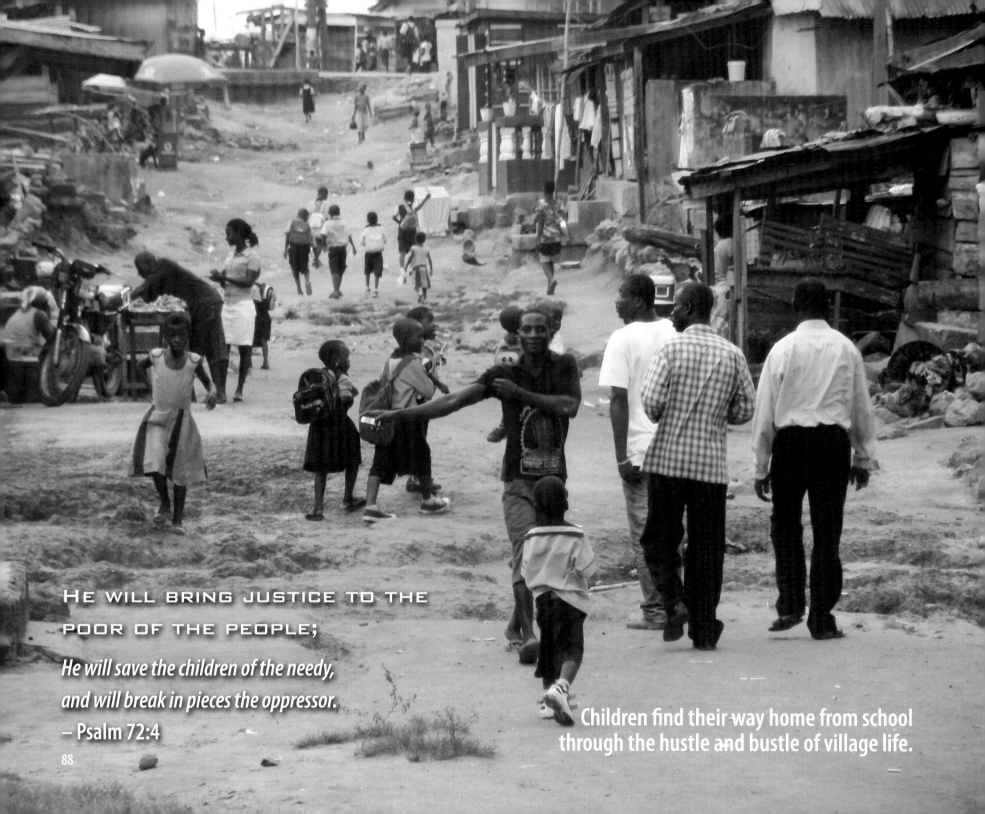

He will bring justice to the poor of the people;

He will save the children of the needy, and will break in pieces the oppressor.
— Psalm 72:4

Children find their way home from school through the hustle and bustle of village life.

88

AFTER YEARS OF WORKING TOGETHER, the king of Gomoa, Ohua, bestowed upon me the great honor of becoming the Development Chief of his village. This position allows me to provide counsel to tribal leadership and champion new opportunities to improve village life. Upon accepting this role, I was given the name of King Akorafutu Omantsimanpong I.

In what was truly a once-in-a-lifetime cultural experience, Cori and I were the guests of honor at a three-day festival filled with authentic dancing, chanting, singing, and eating exotic foods.

This was perhaps the most amazing cultural experiences Cori and I have ever enjoyed together.

It proved to us once again that when your focus is on serving the Lord, He sometimes showers you with blessing, which exceeds anything your mind could have ever imagined.

THEN HE SAID TO THEM,

"The harvest truly is great, but the laborers are few;
therefore pray the Lord of the harvest to send out laborers into His harvest."
– Luke 10:2

I pray this book has given you a glimpse into the people and places Mission Ready is working to serve in Africa. We are humbled that the Lord is using us in this way, yet we know there is so much work left to be done. We invite you to join us in this great adventure by becoming participants in "world evangelization" through your prayers and financial support of Mission Ready's Remote Village Evangelism programs around the world.

ABOUT THE AUTHOR

This book is dedicated to my wife Cori who has been my soul mate, my encourager and my best friend throughout all the great adventures of my life. Her unconditional love and unwavering support have been a great blessing which allowed me to focus on God's calling to build Mission Ready, Inc.

I also dedicate this book to all the Christian missionaries who make sacrifices daily and work tirelessly throughout the world to serve the call Jesus Christ has placed in their hearts.

Finally, I dedicate this book to those visionary supporters of Mission Ready who have embraced the concept of "Remote Village Evangelism" and provided their support through prayers and financial contributions. Without your willingness to to honor God's call to share your time and resources Mission Ready could not accomplish the work it is called to do.

Rob established Mission Ready, Inc. in 2005 in an effort to help Christian men and women understand and plan for the best experience possible while serving the Lord in missionary service, especially those who are indigenous to the countries where they serve. Rob's goal for Mission Ready, Inc. is that it will play a key role in helping at least two thousand future missionaries answer their call to serve. These future missionaries will be able to witness to unreached people groups living in isolated and remote communities.

Mission Ready, Inc. is involved in a number of projects around the world, helping equip indigenous missionaries. This organization has been a part of creating biblical training institutes and community-share microeconomic solutions for tribes and missions organizations—at no cost to the participants.

Rob Morgan draws upon a unique blend of forty years of real world experience leading financial corporations and thirty years of academic experience teaching a wide range of courses in business, finance, and ethics at major universities. He uses these lessons to assist business owners and executive leadership teams in achieving success with integrity. Rob currently teaches at the George Fox University, Indiana Wesleyan University, and Boise State University.

Rob and his wife, Cori, live in Boise, Idaho.

All proceeds from this book go to Mission Ready, Inc., a nonprofit organization. To make a tax deductible donation, visit www.MissionReady.org.
Or, mail your donation to: 967 E, Parkcenter Blvd. Suite 418, Boise, ID 83706.